A Weird History of Science

Crazy Chemistry

John Townsend

Chicago, Illinois

© 2007 Raintree
Published by Raintree,
A division of Reed Elsevier Inc.
Chicago, Illinois

Customer Service 888-363-4266

Visit our website at www.heinemannraintree.com

Produced for Raintree by
Monkey Puzzle Media Ltd.

Designed by Tim Mayer
Printed and bound in China by
South China Printing Company

11 10 09 08 07
10 9 8 7 6 5 4 3 2 1

Library of Congress Cataloging-in-Publication Data
Townsend, John, 1955-

Crazy chemistry / John Townsend.
    p. cm. -- (Weird history of science)
    Includes bibliographical references and index.
    ISBN-13: 978-1-4109-2378-3 (library binding-
hardcover : alk. paper)
    ISBN-13: 978-1-4109-2383-7 (pbk. : alk. paper)
    1. Chemistry--Juvenile literature. I. Title.

QD35.T69 2006
540--dc22

                          2006007031

Acknowledgments

The author and publisher are grateful to the
following for permission to reproduce copyright
material: Advertising Archives p. **43**; AKG-Images
pp. **1**, **5 top** (Erich Lessing), **6** (Dortmund
Westfälisches Schulmuseum), **9**, **11**, **29**, **32**
(Erich Lessing), **40** (Ullstein Bild), **41**; Art
Archive p. **7** (Beijing Institute of Archaeology);
Corbis pp. **5 bottom**, **8** (Christie's Images), **13**
(Chris McLaughlin), **17**, **23** (Bettmann), **35**, **39**
(Bettmann), **42** (Alen MacWeeney); Getty
Images/PhotoDisc **33**, **44**; Heritage Image
Partnership p. **36** (Oxford Science Archive);
Mary Evans Picture Library pp. **21**, **24**; MPM
Images pp. **34** (*The Occupational Diseases*, D.
Appleton & Co, New York, 1914), **48** (Forensic
Consulting); Reuters p. **45**; Science and Society
Picture Library pp. **37**, **46** (Science Museum,
London); Science Photo Library pp. **4** (Sheila
Terry), **5 middle** (Jean-Loup Charmet), **14**, **16**,
18 (Jean-Loup Charmet), **19** (Sheila Terry), **20**,
25, **26** (Sheila Terry), **30** (Charles D. Winters),
31 (Sheila Terry), **47** (Simon Fraser/Pharmacy
Dept., Royal Victoria Hospital, Newcastle), **49**
(Philippe Psaila); Topfoto.co.uk pp. **12**, **15**, **27**
(Image Works), **38**; Wellcome Library, London
pp. **10**, **22**.

Cover photograph of "Mad Professor" Bruce
Lacey reproduced with permission of Getty
Images.

Disclaimer

Contents

Any words appearing in the text in bold,
like this, are explained in the glossary.
You can also look out for them in the
"Word bank" at the bottom of each page.

Risky Science

Science has always tried to find out about the unknown. It has uncovered secrets and challenged what people think, understand, and believe. It has also been full of dangers and deadly mistakes.

Nasty surprises

All throughout history, scientists have had ideas that have made people think twice about what they believe is "fact." This has upset lots of people. For hundreds of years, scientists were imprisoned, tortured, or even put to death, because their ideas went against the religious teachings of the time.

French chemist Antoine Lavoisier (1743–1794) tried to make water by mixing two gases. There were no safety equipment, goggles, or white coats then! Find out how he met a gruesome death on page 17.

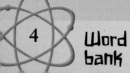

Word bank

apparatus scientific equipment such as test tubes and glass beakers

Ever since scientists first began to ask questions about the world, and look for answers, strange things have happened. By testing ideas and trying out experiments, scientists made weird and wonderful discoveries. Life today would not be the same without the risky work of scientists from the past. They had to find out the hard way that some acids burn flesh, some chemicals suddenly explode, and a single drop of a certain poison kills in an instant.

Daring chemists

In spite of the risks, many scientists bravely kept at their work to find important answers. Sometimes their studies took over their whole lives. That might be why some scientists were seen as strange, because they worked long hours with scary substances and weird **apparatus**.

Many chemists were great thinkers. However, they must have seemed puzzling to others as they locked themselves in their **laboratories** with bubbling mixtures, smelly gases, and fizzing acids. Was the world of chemistry really as crazy as it seemed? Well, you may be surprised to find out just how weird its history could be...

Find out later

Who tried to make gold from boiled urine?

What was so hilarious about this new gas?

How did women risk their lives to make lighting a candle easier?

laboratory scientific work place for experiments, often called a "lab"

In the Beginning

Chemistry is the science that studies all kinds of substances, such as liquids, gases, and powders. It looks at how they change and at the effects they have on other substances. Chemists find out what happens when they mix different substances together. For centuries, chemists tried to make mixtures that could cure diseases, give them long life, or make them rich.

The earliest cave people began a simple kind of chemistry. By mixing ingredients for cooking, medicines, or magic, they found out how substances changed or reacted. When they lit fires and heated certain rocks, they found out about making metals. It was chemistry in the making.

Ancient accidents

Early cave people were probably the first chemists. They discovered how certain kinds of soils reacted with water to make mud and clay for pots. They experimented by boiling various plants, berries, and juices. They risked death because crushed berries and seeds can be dangerous—especially as they didn't know which ones were poisonous.

More than 100,000 years ago, cave people knew how to use fire, heat up rocks and soils, and make colored dyes for their wall paintings.

Word bank

fermenting "brewing" a liquid so that chemical changes turn it into alcohol

Colorful chemistry

Thousands of years ago, people found that different rocks and plants could be crushed to make colorful powders. By adding water, they made paints to decorate pots and produced dyes to color fabrics. When people mixed different powders together to see what new colors they could make, they were doing some of the first chemical experiments.

Ancient pottery jars found in China show that, long ago, people knew how to make rice wine and barley beer. So they knew about the chemical process called **fermenting**. Modern chemists have discovered this by testing the remains of liquids inside jars from 9,000 years ago.

Scientists have discovered the chemical remains of a sweet rice wine made 9,000 years ago. It was found in an ancient jug similar to this one dug up in Henan Province, China.

Ancient Egypt

More than 4,000 years ago, the ancient Egyptians used their knowledge of chemistry to make and shape metals. They dug rocks containing copper, iron, **mercury**, and gold from the ground. They melted these rocks in fires to get out the metals and make precious objects, like crowns. This science produced some of the first great treasures.

mercury heavy, poisonous metal (also called quicksilver) that is liquid at room temperature

Roman and Greek poisons

About 2,000 years ago, many ancient Romans and Greeks studied science and medicine. They experimented with different chemicals to see what effects they had on people's bodies. They became interested in poisons.

Mithradates (136–66 BC), who was king of Pontos (now Turkey), was scared of being poisoned by his main enemies, the Romans. So he tried out various poisons on criminals and tried to make **antidotes** to stop their effects.

Each day, he swallowed small amounts of poison himself, to build up resistance in his body. It all went wrong when the Romans really did attack. The king tried to kill himself with poison and it didn't work, because his body had become resistant. So his guards had to stab him to death instead.

Socrates had to drink deadly poison from the hemlock plant as punishment and died almost immediately.

Word bank   antidote medicine that acts against the effects of poison
corroding eating away

Sorting stuff

One of the greatest Greek thinkers and scientists was Aristotle (384–322 BC). He said that everything was made up of just four **elements**: fire, air, water, and earth. It was a simple idea. However, scientists now know of over 100 substances called pure chemical elements—and fire, air, water, and earth are not among them.

Some ancient Greeks tried to sort substances into groups by tasting them. The groups were salty, sour, sweet, and bitter. Sour-tasting substances led to the word "acid." People found these acidic substances had negative effects, like eating away or **corroding** metals—and burning their tongues!

Chemical dinner

Ancient Romans sometimes slipped poison into the food of an enemy or hated family member. You simply got a deadly mixture from a chemist and added it to the meal. In those days, unlike now, no one could trace the cause of death. The Emperor Caligula kept a stock of different poisons for adding to people's dinners.

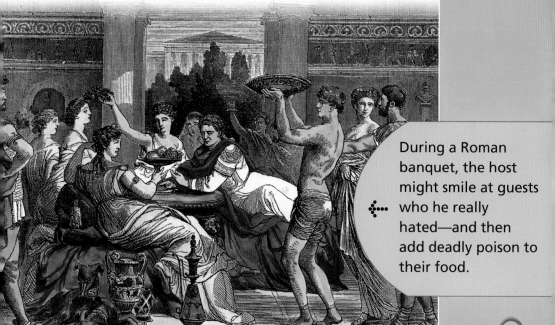

During a Roman banquet, the host might smile at guests who he really hated—and then add deadly poison to their food.

element substance that cannot be broken into simpler substances
hemlock poisonous plant with small white flowers

Medieval magic

About a thousand years ago, across Europe, there was a great interest in witches, spells, and mysterious mixtures. Many people believed it was possible to make powerful juices that could cure illness or bring special powers. Pots and pans bubbled with brews that would give everlasting life to anyone who drank them—or so their makers hoped. The worlds of chemistry and magic were closely mixed.

During the Middle Ages, from about AD 600 to 1500, chemistry was not a real science, as it is today. It was called **alchemy**. Its main aim was to search for special substances to bring health, wealth, and happiness.

Chemical recipes

During medieval times, people who experimented with chemical mixtures started to write down what they did and share their results. These people were alchemists. As they traveled to other countries, they took their "chemical recipes" with them. Ideas about alchemy started to spread far and wide.

This painting by Jan Steen (1626–1679) shows a village alchemist hopefully preparing a new mixture to bring him fame and fortune.

  Word bank   alchemy medieval form of chemistry, especially trying to change ordinary metals into gold

Glorious gold

The most precious substance on Earth, which people have wanted more than any other, is gold. This metal has always been very special. By owning just a small amount, people thought they would become rich and their problems would be over. There was something almost magical about the power of gold.

For hundreds of years, alchemists searched for a substance that would make anything it touched turn into gold. That substance was called the philosopher's stone. A pity no one found it! In time, chemists discovered that gold only occurs naturally. It cannot be made by mixing other substances together.

The endless search

Alchemists searched mainly for two mythical substances: the philosopher's stone and the **elixir** of life. The philosopher's stone was believed to change ordinary metals like iron and lead into gold. The elixir of life was a magical substance that could cure disease and lengthen life. It took centuries to realize that neither substance really existed.

Some people who tried to make medicines and mixtures were accused of being witches. One punishment for this was being dunked in water on a ducking stool.

elixir substance believed to make people live longer or cure disease

Gases

Today, scientists know a great deal about many different gases. Some of them burn, but others don't. Some are light and rise, others are heavier and sink. Some are harmless, others are poisonous. Different gases have all kinds of uses. We know all of this because of chemists and their experiments over the last 400 years.

Robert Boyle

Gases and air fascinated Robert Boyle. He did many experiments to find out about air **pressure**. He proved that air could be squashed by pressure to take up less space. That was an important discovery in the 1600s. Today's scientists still use a scientific law he worked out, called Boyle's Law. Boyle is known as one of the founders of modern chemistry.

Did you know?

Robert Boyle (1627–1691) was born in Ireland, the youngest of 14 children. His father was one of the richest men of the time. Even so, Robert was still interested in making gold and secretly tried to change **mercury** into gold. He became a great scientist and discovered much about gases and air.

In this picture Robert Boyle (right) talks to French scientist Denis Papin about his invention of the air pump.

Word bank

bends sickness in deep-sea divers, when nitrogen bubbles form in blood
expand increase in size or amount

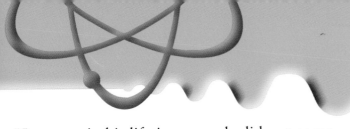

However, in his lifetime, people did not agree with Boyle's ideas. He dared to write that Aristotle was wrong about the four **elements**. Robert tried to prove that any substance can be broken down into smaller particles made of pure chemicals. We now know he was right.

Just so you know

A gas is not solid or liquid. A gas has no shape of its own, and it flows to take up the shape of its container, in a similar way as a liquid such as water. A gas, unlike a liquid, **expands** to fill any larger container, or it can be squashed (pressurized) to fit into a smaller container. If a gas is cooled enough, it changes into a liquid. Gases are all around us in air. The main gases in air are oxygen and nitrogen.

Useful chemistry

Robert Boyle's work with gases made scuba diving possible. In 1667, he noted a condition called "the **bends**" when he experimented with a snake in a jar and an air pump. When lowering the air pressure in the jar, he saw gas bubbles form in the snake's eyes.

Today, scuba divers can swim deep in the ocean with tanks of air on their backs—thanks to the work of Robert Boyle.

pressure pressing force that tries to push or squeeze

Gas discoveries

Robert Boyle insisted on writing down details of his experiments—and changed science. Recording results properly became the new fashion. Experiments with gases were carefully written down so that other chemists could continue the work.

About 100 years after Boyle, Henry Cavendish developed ways of collecting gases and studying them. He discovered a new gas, called **hydrogen**, by collecting it in a "gas bag" over a water tank. This gas bag method was then used to collect other gases.

Henry Cavendish kept lots of notes, but published very few scientific reports. He did not care at all about being famous. ⋯⋮▸

Just so you know

Hydrogen is the lightest of all gases. It burns easily and has no smell or color. It was once used to fill balloons, airships, and other lighter-than-air craft. This was very risky, because one spark can make hydrogen burst into flames. In fact, some hydrogen-filled airships had terrible accidents when they caught fire. We now use a safer, light gas called helium instead of hydrogen.

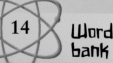
eccentric acting or thinking in an unusual way

Strange ways

Henry Cavendish was a good chemist, but people found him strange. He was so shy he hardly spoke to anyone. He hated crowds and hardly ever left his house, carrying out all his work in his home **laboratory.**

As well as working with gas-filled balloons, Cavendish did many other experiments. He discovered the dangerous chemical nitric acid, and worked out a way of measuring the weight of the whole Earth. He also measured the strength of an electric current by passing it through his body as a shock and noting how much it hurt. That was dangerous science!

More than 100 years after Cavendish's work, the giant Zeppelin airships were filled with hydrogen gas.

hydrogen lightest of all pure chemical substances, a gas that easily catches fire

A matter of life and death

If we don't breathe in, we do not get the vital gas oxygen from the air into our bodies—and we die. If we don't breathe out, we do not get rid of the poisonous gas **carbon dioxide**, which is made in the body. Three centuries ago, no one knew about oxygen and how important it is for life, or that carbon dioxide could be deadly.

As well as discovering several new gases, Joseph Priestley also carried out experiments on electricity and light.

Word bank

carbon dioxide heavy gas that puts out flames, and is made by the body as a waste gas that must be breathed out

Joseph Priestley (1733–1804) was not a trained scientist. However, as he dabbled in chemistry, he made big discoveries about oxygen. His experiments involved putting plants under water, burning candles in different gases, and keeping mice without much air. He was the first person to study the **respiration** of plants—the way that they "breathe" like animals by taking in oxygen and giving off carbon dioxide.

The gas man

Joseph Priestley lived next to a brewery and was puzzled by the gas coming from the **fermenting** barrels. He found that this "brewery gas" put out flames. He also noticed that it sank to the ground. He made more of it in his lab at home. When he bubbled it through water, he drank some and liked it. He'd invented carbonated drinks! The gas was later called carbon dioxide.

One of Priestley's later experiments produced a new gas called nitrous oxide. People soon found that this gas did weird things, as you can read on page 18.

as you can read on page 18.

What became of the "Oxygen Chemists"?

- 1786 Scheele died from breathing in too many deadly gases like **cyanide**, which he also tasted in his experiments!
- 1794 Lavoisier was beheaded during the French Revolution because ordinary people resented his wealth.
- 1794 Joseph Priestley fled from England to the United States because his house was burned down by mobs who hated his political views.

Plants such as trees use oxygen, like animals. When they soak up light energy, they also make and release oxygen, which keeps the air fresh.

cyanide deadly poison that can be a powder, salt, liquid, or gas
respiration when living things take in oxygen and release carbon dioxide

What a laugh!

When Joseph Priestley first made the gas nitrous oxide in 1793, he wondered what it could be used for. He noticed it had no color and no smell. Yet when he sniffed it, he couldn't help laughing! He had created "laughing gas." Anyone who breathed in the gas felt light-headed or dizzy and giggled.

This cartoon from the early 1800s shows Humphry Davy (at the back on the right) helping a chemist to show the effects of laughing gas.

Secrets of nitrous oxide

Humphry Davy gave nitrous oxide gas to visitors at his lab and was amazed that many started laughing. Today, the gas is used in various processes instead of the chemicals called **CFCs** that can damage the **ozone layer** high above the Earth.

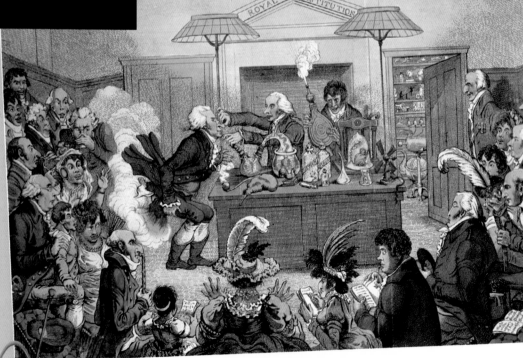

Word bank

CFCs chemicals that harm Earth's atmosphere, once used in spray cans and refrigerators

The young scientist Humphry Davy (1778–1829) took a sniff of the gas in 1799. He said: "My sensations were pleasant. It was as if I had a small dose of wine. I began to move and to feel merry." Davy tried it out on his friends— just for a laugh.

Giggle gas

News of laughing gas's funny effects soon spread. The poet Robert Southey wrote: "I am sure the air in heaven must be this wonder-working gas of delight." Before long, people began holding parties where they sniffed nitrous oxide to make everyone giggly. They did not realize the risks, as the gas can make people giddy, lose control, fall over, and damage their lungs. Some people even died from breathing too much. It was no longer a laughing matter. However the gas soon found a serious use in medicine, as you can read on the next page.

Humphry Davy tested his safety lamp in coal mines in the early 1800s, and it went into general use in 1815.

Did you know?

Humphry Davy saved lives of many coal m because of his inter gases. Explosions ir mines used to kill workers because th flames of their torc set off a gas callec methane, which c underground and catch fire. Humph designed his spec lamp so that it w explode the gas.

ozone layer gas layer high above Earth that blocks out most of the Sun's harmful ultraviolet (UV) rays

Killing pain

An American dentist named Horace Wells (1815–1848) was amazed to see people rolling with laughter at a show. They were taking breaths of a new gas just for fun. They bumped into things, but didn't seem to feel pain. This got Wells thinking. Would this "laughing gas" help him in his work? After all, it was always bad news when he had to strap down patients to pull out their teeth as they screamed in agony. Now there might be a way to make patients relax and even smile as their teeth came out!

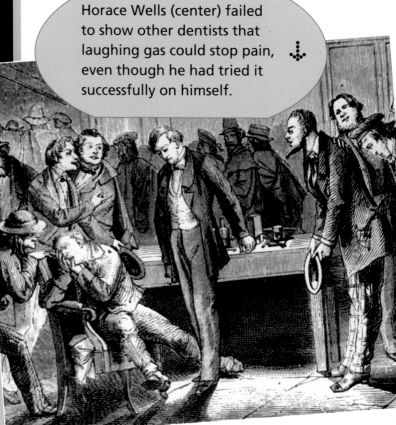

Horace Wells (center) failed to show other dentists that laughing gas could stop pain, even though he had tried it successfully on himself.

Word bank

addicted relying on regular use of a substance such as a drug, so that it becomes almost impossible to stop

Oops—wrong dose

Horace Wells was so sure that laughing gas would help his patients, he took a sniff of it and pulled out one of his own teeth. It didn't hurt. So he decided to demonstrate the gas to medical students at the Massachusetts Hospital, in Boston.

In 1845, Wells gave a patient a breath of laughing gas and pulled out his tooth while everyone watched. But the patient yelped in pain—he hadn't been given enough. The crowd hissed and booed. Poor Horace was a public failure. In spite of this false start, nitrous oxide was soon being used in medicine as an **anesthetic** to deaden pain. However, Wells was ruined by his failed demonstration and ended his own life three years later.

Crazy end

While Horace Wells v studying gases such nitrous oxide and **chloroform**, he bec **addicted** to them. began to affect his He became violent was put in Tombs Prison in New York While there, he kil himself with a fina dose of chlorofor

Wells died in a bathtub after breathing in chloroform, a gas he had studied for many years.

anesthetic substance that numbs part or all of the body, or causes a deep sleep
chloroform colorless, poisonous chemical that causes sleep in small doses

Chemistry on the operating table

In the 1840s, a Scottish surgeon named Robert Liston (1794–1847) was famous for cutting off patients' diseased limbs at high speed. He would press the blood vessels closed with his powerful left hand while sawing off the leg or arm with his right. It was said that when he began to cut, anyone who blinked missed the operation. He was so quick, that once he accidentally cut off his assistant's fingers.

There were no pain-killing **anesthetics** at this time. One patient of Liston's was so scared that he jumped off the operating table, ran along the hall, and locked himself in a bathroom. Liston chased after him, pushed down the door, and carried him back for his operation.

Magic fumes

For many years, people knew that the chemical ether made them drowsy when they breathed its fumes. It wasn't until 1842 that an American surgeon, Crawford Long, used ether as an anesthetic. As he operated on the neck of a sleeping patient, those watching accused him of magic and threatened to hang him!

Crawford Williamson Long (1815–1878) carried out several operations from 1842 using "sulfuric ether" to numb the senses of his patients.

Word bank

antiseptics chemicals that kill germs such as bacteria
ether liquid giving off fumes that were once used as an anesthetic

Chemistry to the rescue

In 1846, Robert Liston was the first surgeon to remove a patient's leg using **ether** as an anesthetic. When the patient woke up, he asked Liston: "When are you going to begin? Take me back, I can't have it done." He had no idea the operation had finished. Liston claimed that the new discovery beat all the older methods.

From the 1850s, pain-free surgery became more common because of anesthetic chemicals. However, in times of war, there were never enough of these chemicals. Injured soldiers still had to have wounded legs or arms cut off while they screamed in pain.

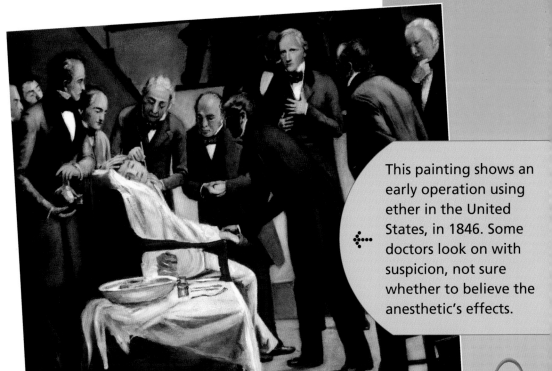

This painting shows an early operation using ether in the United States, in 1846. Some doctors look on with suspicion, not sure whether to believe the anesthetic's effects.

Sudden sleep

In the 1840s, patients who breathed in gas or fumes before an operation were at risk. If they breathed in too much, they might never wake up. If they didn't breathe enough, they would wake up during the operation. So patients still screamed, or died, on the operating table.

Scientists were eager to improve **anesthetics**. They continued to experiment with chemicals that could put patients to sleep safely. James Simpson, a Scottish surgeon, was worried about the risks of **ether**, which often made patients cough badly. In 1847, he began trying various chemicals on himself. He often woke up on the floor!

After James Simpson tried chloroform on himself, he passed out and was found on the floor by a friend. It worked!

inhaler device used for breathing in medicines through the mouth or nose

Taking risks

One night, James Simpson and his two assistants sat down to a dangerous experiment in his dining room. They sniffed different gases without much effect until they tried a small bottle of **chloroform**. They all breathed it in—and passed out. When Simpson woke he said: "This is far stronger and better than ether." He then began to use chloroform on patients in operations.

Other doctors tried chloroform, but some patients died because they breathed in too much. Many people said that it was bad. Then, in 1853, Queen Victoria used it when she gave birth to her seventh child. Chloroform became the new respectable fashion.

The lead mask of this chloroform inhaler was molded to the patient's face. On breathing in, the air inside the mask filled with chloroform.

...ying with Fire

reminder

...nt Greeks
...re was one of
...**elements** that,
...th earth, water,
...made up
...ng. However, fire
...chemical or a
...ce. It is part of an
...releasing
...al reaction
...n the gas oxygen
...**uel** such as
...or coal.

For thousands of years, people tried to understand, control, and use fire. In ancient times, forest fires started by lightning would cause terror for everyone around. Even today, fires still kill thousands of people every year.

When flames could be controlled and used for light, heat, and cooking, then fire also became a lifesaver. And it became a powerful tool for heating and molding metals, pottery, glass, and bricks. Fire has been a major force in human history and an important part of science. Many discoveries were made when people learned to use heat, sparks, and flames in their labs.

Almost half a million years ago, early people learned to control fire for warmth, cooking, frightening away wild animals—and simple science.

Word bank

fuel substance that burns to give out useful amounts of energy, usually light and/or heat

Using flames

Chemistry has always depended on heat to change substances. Flames enabled people to heat certain rocks and get out pure metals, to harden or "fire" clay into pottery, and to heat sand so much that it became glass.

Long ago, the big challenges were to make fire and to keep it alight for a long time. Until the 1800s, lighting a fire was a major task. Today, we simply strike a match. Matches and many other fiery devices only came about because of some strange chemistry. As you can read next, it was truly explosive science.

Flames in chemistry

Most chemistry labs always have a flame ready for experiments. The Bunsen burner has been a part of science for more than 150 years. It was named after the German chemist Robert Bunsen (1811–1899). He improved the original design made by English scientist Michael Faraday.

Bunsen burners are important tools today in school science lessons. However, they get very hot and must always be treated with care.

27

Sparks and flashes

In spite of huge risks, scientists have always been interested in sparks, flashes, and bangs. They wanted to know: "Why do some things burn while others don't?" Some chemicals not only burned, they flared up suddenly with great power and a loud BANG. The next question was: Why do some substances explode?

Fireworks

Black powder, also known as gunpowder, is a mixture of sulfur, carbon, and other chemicals. It was first used in China about a thousand years ago to make simple fireworks. By the 1500s, Italian scientists were making more spectacular fireworks using different mixes of gunpowder. By the 1600s, firework parties became popular among rich people in Europe and America.

Until the 1830s, nearly all fireworks flashed and fizzed in shades of orange or showered white sparks. However, Italian chemists wanted more. They added different powders and substances called metallic salts to make reds, greens, blues, and yellows. Big-time firework displays had arrived. Powders that exploded in different colors of smoke were not just pretty to watch. They soon became used for weapons, as you can read on later pages.

Off with a bang

In about 1350, a German alchemist called Berthold Schwarz was probably the first person to use gunpowder to shoot objects up into the air. He may even have developed the first cannon. It is thought that he was killed by one of his own explosions.

Just so you know

An explosive is a substance that turns from a solid or liquid chemical into a gas. This suddenly gets bigger or **expands** and causes huge **pressure** on its surroundings. The pressure can hurl a ball out of a cannon or shoot a bullet from a gun.

Berthold Schwarz, a monk, did many experiments with gunpowder. He tried setting off a gunpowder charge with a spark from a piece of flint to shoot a block into the air.

Gunpowder in the 1600s

Scientists found many uses for gunpowder, such as blasting holes in rocks for mines, and later making canals and tunnels.

- 1670 Gunpowder was first used in the tin mines of Cornwall, England.
- 1675 The first gunpowder factory was built in Milton, Massachusetts.
- 1696 The first recorded use of gunpowder for building roads was in Switzerland.

There are two types of chemical explosives—low and high. Low explosives, like gunpowder, take a few thousandths of a second to blow up—which for a chemical change can be quite slow! High explosives are different. A **shock wave** zips through the chemical at incredible speed. The explosion happens in a few millionths of a second, with sudden and massive power.

High explosives

Scientists who worked with explosives often got badly hurt. In 1811, the French chemist Pierre Dulong (1785–1838) was experimenting with various chemicals and suddenly— BOOM! Dulong lost an eye and fingers in the explosion, but he still didn't give up his work.

When the metal potassium touches water, it burns very fast with a blinding light.

Did you know?

Some chemicals react together very fast and violently. **Potassium** does this with water, which Humphry Davy discovered in 1807. He threw some potassium into water and it "skimmed about with a hissing sound, and soon burned with a lovely purple light." Humphry apparently danced with joy at his discovery.

Word bank

potassium soft, silver-white, lightweight metal that catches fire if it touches water

Repeat performance

News of Dulong's accident reached the English chemist Humphry Davy. He decided to copy the experiment using a tiny amount of a chemical called nitrogen chloride, the size of this "O." It exploded in Davy's face. After removing broken glass from his eye, Davy wrote to Dulong: "The oil which you mentioned made me curious, but I nearly lost my eye."

Davy was not happy to leave things there. He did more experiments with even more of the chemical nitrogen chloride. His assistant, Michael Faraday, wrote: "It stood for a moment and then exploded with a fearful noise." Ouch!

Lucky escape

In 1812, Michael Faraday described an experiment with his boss Davy. "Both Humphry and I had masks on, but I escaped the best. Humphry had his face cut in two places around the chin, and a violent blow on the forehead struck through thick leather. He has decided to finish with this experiment for the time being."

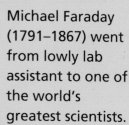

Michael Faraday (1791–1867) went from lowly lab assistant to one of the world's greatest scientists.

shock wave sudden burst of energy that travels very quickly

Urine to matches

A strange accident of chemistry changed the way of making fire for ever. A German alchemist called Hennig Brand was boiling mixtures in his endless search to make gold. One day, in 1669, he must have run out of ideas because he started to boil **urine** in a pan! Something weird happened. The urine mixture boiled down to a paste, which Brand made into a waxy substance. To his surprise, it glowed in the dark. He was the first person to make **phosphorus**.

This painting shows Hennig Brand in 1669 discovering a curious glowing substance that would be named phosphorus.

32

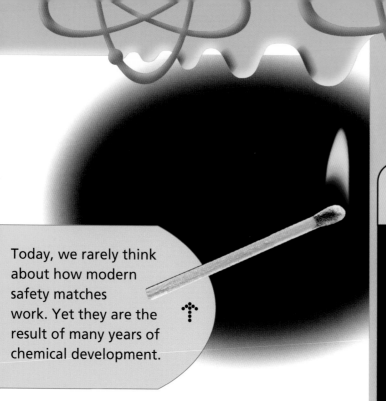

Today, we rarely think about how modern safety matches work. Yet they are the result of many years of chemical development.

Stick of fire

Later, in 1826, a British chemist named John Walker was stirring a mixture of chemicals with a stick. The chemicals formed a dried lump on the end of the stick. When he scraped this against the floor to get rid of the lump, it burst into flames. He'd made a giant match! He tipped small splints of wood with this mixture and began selling them as "friction matches."

A problem was that these new matches shot out sparks and had a terrible smell. They could also catch fire by accident—in the United States, they were kept in metal safes. Then came an answer. The substance phosphorus, as discovered by Brand, was added to the match heads. This made them work far better.

urine waste liquid passed out of the body, usually pale yellow

Glowing jaws to exploding aprons

From the end of the 1830s, millions of matches were made in factories. Tons of white **phosphorus** went into all the match heads. However, no one knew this chemical was deadly. The workers had to suck the ends of the matches to finish them properly. They soon got toothaches and swollen gums. In time, their jaws puffed up and oozed with pus. This terrible condition was known as "phossy jaw."

People's jawbones rotted away and actually glowed greenish-white in the dark. The face became red and sore, and infection could set in. Smelly green fluid, pus, oozed from holes in the skin. If the jaw wasn't removed by an operation, the patient died. In fact, phosphorus was so deadly that small children who ate match heads by accident were often killed.

White phosphorus on match heads gave people "phossy jaw" where the jaw rotted away. Talking and eating were difficult, and infection by germs often took hold.

Word bank

guncotton mild explosive often used in firework rockets

Many women and children worked in match factories in the 1870s and became very sick from chemical poisoning due to phosphorus.

Chemistry in the kitchen

The wife of German chemist Christian Schonbein told him not to do experiments at home. But he did so when she went out. In 1845, he spilled a mixture of acids and rushed to clear up the mess. He grabbed his wife's cotton apron to mop up and hung it over the stove to dry.

Suddenly, the apron burst into flames and disappeared in a flash. Luckily, Schonbein's wife wasn't wearing it at the time! Even so, he must have had some explaining to do. What he'd invented was **guncotton**, an explosive that soon became famous as the exciting new "smokeless gunpowder."

insane very sick state of mind

A big noise in chemistry

Italian chemist Ascanio Sobrero discovered a new high explosive in 1847. It was a yellow oil called **nitroglycerine**. It was so powerful that if he put a single drop on the table and hit it with a hammer, it would explode and blow the hammer's head off its handle.

Sobrero was badly injured in one of his nitroglycerine explosions, and his face was scarred. Even so, he carried on his work and went to see Swedish chemist Alfred Nobel. In the 1860s, Alfred and his father set up a factory to make nitroglycerine. However, a terrible surprise was in store.

Flood Rock was a danger to ships entering New York Harbor. In 1885, chemists used dynamite to blow it up, in one of the biggest explosions ever seen.

Word bank

dynamite   rock-blasting explosive made from nitroglycerine
gelignite   explosive that cannot blow up without a detonator

A booming industry

In 1864, the Nobel factory blew up, killing Alfred's brother and four other people. The Swedish Government was so worried about nitroglycerine that it would not let Nobel rebuild his factory in the same place. Instead, he started making nitroglycerine on a floating factory in the middle of a lake. He mixed the dangerous nitroglycerine with clay to make it safer—and invented another explosive, **dynamite**. Then, by mixing nitroglycerine with **guncotton**, he went on to invent **gelignite**.

Alfred Nobel became very rich and famous for his explosive discoveries. He made a great difference to mining and rock-blasting. Safe-blowers had him to thank, as well!

Alfred Nobel (1833–1896) made a lot of money from inventing explosions that could be used for killing. However, he put the money to good use with the Nobel Prizes.

nitroglycerine oily, explosive, poisonous liquid used to make dynamite

Deadly Chemistry

Records from long ago show how harmful chemicals were used in warfare. In ancient Greece, Solon of Athens added poison to the drinking water of the enemy. In the 1400s, the great inventor Leonardo da Vinci suggested that missiles filled with **arsenic** powder would make a good weapon.

Science and the whole world were changed by the amazing inventions and discoveries of chemists, using gases, fires, and explosives. Homes, hospitals, and factories were all helped by the great work done in the last 200 years. But there was a downside. As well as helping people and saving lives, chemistry now had the power to kill people in the thousands. In times of war, the horrors of chemistry were now greatly feared.

Trying to poison enemies goes back thousands of years. Yet the term "chemical warfare" was first used in 1917. It means using mixtures or gases to burn, poison, or choke the enemy.

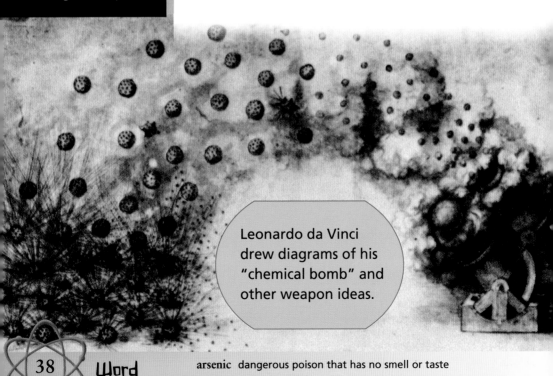

Leonardo da Vinci drew diagrams of his "chemical bomb" and other weapon ideas.

Word bank   arsenic dangerous poison that has no smell or taste

Almost a chemical war

The American Civil War started in 1861. The Union states of the North and the Confederate states of the South disagreed about how to run the country. During the four years of warfare, both sides had planned to use chemicals.

A New York City teacher, John Doughty, suggested firing shells (strong containers) filled with liquid **chlorine** to cover the enemy with harmful chlorine gas. Confederates planned to fire gas bombs over the Union troops. In the end, for various reasons, no chemical weapons were used. If they had been, the total of 600,000 dead soldiers could have been far higher.

A cunning plan

In the 1860s, American teacher John Doughty said of his chemical cannon idea:
"If the shell should explode over the heads of the enemy, the gas would rapidly fall to the ground. The men could not dodge it. They could then be disarmed and captured as though both their legs were broken."

In the Civil War, Union soldiers planned to fire containers of deadly chemicals from this massive cannon.

chlorine heavy, greenish-yellow, harmful gas, often used as a liquid in bleach

39

Killer gas

There were more deaths caused by chemicals in the last century than at any time before. The terrible fact was that much gas poisoning was deliberate, not accidental.

In World War I (1914–1918), thousands of shells filled with chemicals were fired at the enemy. The shells exploded and released gases that harmed the lungs of the troops. At first, the shells contained too much explosive, which seemed to destroy the chemicals. A German scientist, Fritz Haber, had the idea of making a cloud of poisonous gas by using shells filled with **chlorine**. These were used in 1915 during the battle for Ypres, France. Another terrible chemical weapon was mustard gas. It caused blisters, burns, choking, and blindness.

Apart from working on chemical weapons, Fritz Haber (1868–1934) also worked on machines to get rid of dangerous gases in coal mines.

Just so you know

Mustard gas is a yellow, oily liquid at ordinary temperatures. Poured out of its sealed container, it gives off enough gas to kill. It got its name from the mustardlike smell when it blew over the soldiers in World War I.

Word bank

pesticide chemical used to kill harmful pests, especially insects such as flies or beetles

Sarin

Sarin was a deadly chemical developed in Germany as a **pesticide** in 1938. As a gas, it has no smell. Once it gets into the lungs and blood, it soon stops the heart. As a gas, Sarin can kill with just a few breaths. As a liquid, one tiny drop on the skin is deadly in minutes. It is one of the most feared chemical weapons.

Soldiers and their mules and horses had to use gas masks, to protect them from chemical weapons in World War I.

Tear gas

Tear gas is sometimes fired into rioting crowds to stop the violence. The name "tear gas" is used for a group of chemicals that make people feel very uncomfortable. The gas can cause the eyes to water or go blind for a short time, as well as bring on coughing and a feeling of nausea.

In spite of the scary chemistry of war over the last hundred years, chemists have also made some wonderful discoveries. They continue to work on many mind-boggling projects. Just one of the huge chemical advances is plastics.

Before 1900, no one could imagine how many materials could be made out of dark, sticky oil from the ground. The idea of wearing clothes made from chemicals found in oil, or petroleum, would seem totally crazy. Yet many of the fabrics and fashions people wear now have come straight from the **petrochemical** industry.

Yesterday's plastic

The word "plastic" means "able to be shaped and molded." It was first used to describe a human-made material in 1862 when an English scientist, Alexander Parkes, tried to make a cheap type of rubber from plant material. His invention was "Parksine" but no one took much interest in it at the time.

From the 1920s, millions of radios, clocks, and other objects had cases made from Bakelite.

Word bank

cellophane thin, see-through material used as a wrapping
petrochemical chemical obtained from oil (petroleum) or natural gas

Brand new science

When a Swiss scientist saw a waiter spill wine that stained a tablecloth, he thought how useful a wipe-clean coating on the cloth would be. The scientist was Jacques Brandenberger and he set about making a clear layer or film to coat cloth. In the early 1900s, he tried different chemicals but none worked very well. However, one of his results found another use—**cellophane**. This was the first human-made waterproof wrapping material, just right for packaging.

The first hard plastic material was made in 1907 by a New York chemist, Leo Baekeland. He called his new material Bakelite. It did not burn or melt, it was tough, and it did not carry electricity. It was just right for the cases of electrical goods.

In the 1940s, stockings made from the plastic-type material nylon became so popular that the stockings themselves were known as "nylons."

Nylon

Clothes were always made from natural fibers like wool, silk, and cotton—until machines started spinning threads made from chemicals in oil. The plastics craze of the 1920s led clothes-makers to find cheaper fibers. In 1939, the silk in stockings was replaced by a new human-made fabric called nylon. It seemed like a crazy idea, but it soon caught on.

Present for the future —

To the clamorous suggestions for Christmas gifting may we add another still, small voice? May we whisper that "Bear Brand" Stockings offer the infallible solution to this youthful old problem? The cost of winning your friend's undying gratitude lies anywhere between 3/11 and 6/11, so little in fact, that we wouldn't blame you giving yourself a Bear Brand gift. And, let us add, who is more worthy?

43

Plastic times

Where would we be today without substances like plastic, polyethylene, and nylon? They are now probably the most-used materials in homes, factories, stores, and vehicles. Modern chemistry is improving these materials all the time.

Plastics and fibers like polyethylene are **polymers**—substances made up of long rows of the same chemical units, joined like links in a chain. Polymer plastics are making all kinds of science possible for the first time. They are in electrical goods such as cell phones and laptop computers, making them smaller and lighter. On the other hand, larger goods like refrigerators and dishwashers last longer because the plastics in them do not rust or rot. Chemists continue to make even more types of plastic in the 21st century.

Millions of uses

Plastics today can be soft and flexible, or rigid and hard. They can be made into any shape. The plastic sheet of a modern shopping bag is one-third as thick as it was 30 years ago—yet stronger. Many plastics can be recycled, or they rot away naturally after use. That's called "green chemistry."

Chemists from long ago probably never imagined that oil could make so many products, from paints and fuels to fibers for clothing.

Word bank

polymer substance made of many identical chemical units linked together

The way ahead

Plastics were once weak and cracked easily. But now they could make a whole car! Strong plastics can be poured into molds to make parts that simply slot together. The car's rustproof body is said to withstand everyday knocks, such as a bash from a bicycle or car door—without a dent. New plastic clip-on replacement parts should be far cheaper than those for other cars. Plastic cars are far lighter than metal cars, too, so they can go faster and need less fuel. Maybe all cars will be plastic one day.

The planned Think car is made almost entirely of plastic and is light, strong, and rustproof.

Saving lives

Many chemists today work on the search for new medicines and drugs. Without chemistry, we would all have many more headaches. One of the best-known medical drugs is aspirin. Billions of aspirin pills are swallowed each year to kill pain. Another chemical in aspirin is thought to save thousands of lives by preventing heart attacks and **strokes**. Since 1969, astronauts have taken aspirin pills into space, to treat the headaches and muscle pains caused by space travel.

Just so you know

For hundreds of years, people chewed a type of willow plant because it helped to relieve pain. Chemists found that a substance called salicin in the bark was the painkiller. They worked out ways of making it in the **laboratory**. This is how aspirin began.

Did you know?

In 1897, Felix Hoffmann, a chemist at Germany's Bayer Company, made a powder from an acid called ASA. It was used to help his father's painful limbs. The powder was mixed in water and drunk—and it worked. This was aspirin. Bayer made the first aspirin tablets in 1915. Children's chewable aspirin tablets were first made in 1952.

For almost a hundred years, aspirin has been one of the most common medicines around the world.

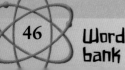
Word bank

chemotherapy use of chemicals to treat and control diseases such as cancers

Fighting cancer

One way of treating cancer patients today is with chemicals. This is called **chemotherapy**. The drugs used for chemotherapy were once made from chemicals in plants. One drug, called Taxol, was made in 1993 from the bark of a type of yew tree.

Today, most anti-cancer drugs are made by chemists. These drugs aim to damage the cancer growths but not healthy body parts. Such drugs can cure some types of cancer and limit the spread of others, although they may have side-effects such as hair loss. Many scientists think that cures for all cancers will be possible in the future.

Achievement of the century

Scientists could be on the verge of developing a cancer-preventing substance, or **vaccine**, that will save millions of lives each year. It is expected that new chemical drugs will slow cancer growths, or stop them from starting, or protect the body against them. Billions of dollars are spent each year on cancer research.

Chemists who specialize in medical drugs are called pharmacists. These pharmacists are preparing drugs used for chemotherapy.

stroke sudden illness caused by lack of blood to the brain, usually due to a blood clot
vaccine injection to produce protection or immunity to a particular disease

Science fact and fiction

News stories are full of far-fetched chemistry in action. What people think might be crazy science fiction may well be science fact. For example, can you believe that a new type of car paint makes scratches disappear after a few days? If a stone flies up and chips the car, the scratch automatically heals—just like our skin!

Chemistry keeps catching murderers. A killer may scrub the murder scene clean after getting rid of the dead body. Then the police arrive with a chemical called Luminol. One spray of this shows blood, even in what seems to be a spotless room. Luminol makes tiny specks of blood glow in the dark.

When Luminol is sprayed at a murder scene, it makes any traces of blood glow blue.

forensics use of science to investigate facts and establish what really happened

Real science

The real world of science is very different from the view we see in movies and on television. The lonely chemist, working secretly in a dusty lab with bubbling mixtures, has long gone. Today's chemists work as big teams in huge research centers and factories. They are employed in many different industries, from making medicines to building skyscrapers.

Chemistry is part of all our lives. It makes paints, dyes, cosmetics, perfumes, and plastics. Farming and food production, as well as crime **forensics**, all depend on the skills of chemists. They have come a long way from those risky experiments with gases and poisons. We owe much of today's knowledge to the amazing chemists of history and their once-daring ideas.

Smelling substances may seem like a strange way to make a living—but it's all part of the modern not-so-crazy world of chemistry.

Chemistry Timeline

About 350 BC	Ancient Greeks such as Aristotle believe that all matter belonged to one of four **elements**: earth, air, water, or fire
About 1000–1650	**Alchemists** try to change lead and other metals to gold, as well as discover an **elixir** for everlasting health
1660s	Robert Boyle makes important discoveries about gases and gas laws. He was the first to imagine that small particles (now known as atoms) could combine to form different substances
1669	German alchemist Hennig Brand discovers **phosphorus**
1766	Henry Cavendish discovers **hydrogen** gas and begins the detailed recording of science experiments
1770s	Joseph Priestley discovers oxygen, carbon monoxide, and nitrous oxide
1770s	Carl Scheele discovers **chlorine**, tartaric acid, and oxidation of metals (how they combine with oxygen)
1779	Antoine Lavoisier gives oxygen its name. He also discovers nitrogen, and studies acids and many other chemicals
1790s	Humphry Davy begins many ideas of electro-chemistry and studies different gases and explosions
Early 1800s	Michael Faraday proves that gases can be changed into liquids, which he did with chlorine. He also makes huge progress in the science of electricity

1842	Crawford Long, American surgeon, first uses **ether** as an **anesthetic**
1845	Horace Wells, American dentist, first uses nitrous oxide gas as an anesthetic
1847	James Simpson, surgeon, experiments with **chloroform** as an anesthetic
1867	Alfred Nobel invents **dynamite**, smokeless gunpowder, and blasting **gelignite**. He establishes international awards for achievements in chemistry, physics, and medicine
1907	Leo Baekeland invents the first real plastic, which is the first completely human-made resin substance, Bakelite
1920	The **polymer** fiber called polyester is made from chemicals
1960	Wilard Libby (1908–1980) wins the Nobel Prize for developing carbon-dating as a way to find the age of many materials
1997	Chrysler introduces the CCV "concept car" made almost entirely of plastic
2000	Alan Heeger, Alan MacDiarmid, and Hideki Shirakawa receive the Nobel Prize for discovering new plastic-type substances that can carry electricity, called conductive **polymers**
2004	Scientists create two new "superheavy" chemical elements (pure substances), numbers 113 and 115

Find Out More

Are chemists happy?

Chemistry may be risky, crazy, and even deadly, but it can also be a life-long passion. In 1667, German chemist Johann Joachim Becher wrote: "Chemists are a strange class of people who seek their pleasures amongst smoke and vapor, soot and flames, poison and poverty. Yet amongst all these evils, I seem to live so sweetly that I would rather die than change places with a king."

Using the Internet

Explore the Internet to find out more about the history of chemistry or to see pictures of famous scientists and experiments.

You can use a search engine such as
www.yahooligans.com

Or ask a question at
www.ask.com

Type in key words such as
- alchemy
- Humphry Davy
- anesthetics
- Alfred Nobel
- plastics

You can find an exciting introduction to the science of chemistry at
www.chem4kids.com/

There are useful summaries of various chemical processes at
www.chemistry.org/kids

Books

You can find out more about strange science and weird chemistry by looking at other books or searching the Internet.

Arnold, Nick. *Horrible Science: Chemical Chaos* (New York: Scholastic Books, 1997)

Baldwin, Carol. *Material Matters: Acids and Bases* (Chicago: Raintree, 2004)

Baldwin, Carol. *Material Matters: Chemical Reactions* (Chicago: Raintree, 2004)

Parker, Steve. *Tabletop Scientist: Air* (Chicago: Raintree, 2005)

Townsend, John. *A Painful History of Medicine: Pills, Powders & Potions* (Chicago: Raintree, 2005)

News flash: live 20 years longer!

Science may be about to let people live far longer. By the year 2050, some people may be taking anti-aging medical drugs that increase the human life span by 20 years or more. Scientists in California are working on the new drugs, which could come into use for some people as early as 2010. Celebrating your 100th birthday may become almost normal, rather than the rare occasion it is today.

Internet search tips

There are billions of pages on the Internet so it can be difficult to find exactly what you are looking for.

These search tips will help you find websites more quickly:

- Know exactly what you want to find out about first.
- Use two to six keywords in a search, putting the most important words first.
- Be precise. Only use names of people, places, or things.

Glossary

addicted relying on regular use of a substance such as a drug, so that it becomes almost impossible to stop

alchemy medieval form of chemistry, especially trying to change ordinary metals into gold

anesthetic substance that numbs part or all of the body, or causes a deep sleep

antidote medicine that acts against the effects of poison

antiseptics chemicals that kill germs such as bacteria

apparatus scientific equipment such as test tubes and glass beakers

arsenic dangerous poison that has no smell or taste

bends sickness in deep-sea divers, when nitrogen bubbles form in blood

carbon dioxide heavy gas that puts out flames, and is made by the body as a waste gas that must be breathed out

cellophane thin, see-through material used as a wrapping

CFCs (chlorofluorocarbons) chemicals that harm Earth's atmosphere, once used in spray cans and refrigerators

chemotherapy use of chemicals to treat and control diseases such as cancers

chlorine heavy, greenish-yellow, harmful gas, often used as a liquid in bleach

chloroform colorless, poisonous chemical that causes sleep in small doses

corroding eating away

cyanide deadly poison that can be a powder, salt, liquid, or gas

dynamite rock-blasting explosive made from nitroglycerine

eccentric acting or thinking in an unusual way

element substance that cannot be broken into simpler substances

elixir substance believed to make people live longer or cure disease

ether liquid giving off fumes that were once used as an anesthetic

expand increase in size or amount

fermenting "brewing" a liquid so that chemical changes turn it into alcohol

forensics use of science to investigate facts and establish what really happened

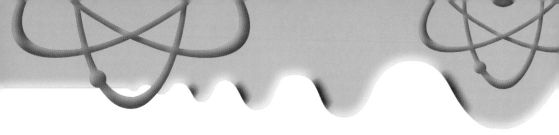

fuel substance that burns to give out useful amounts of energy, usually light and/or heat

gelignite explosive that cannot blow up without a detonator

guncotton mild explosive often used in fireworks rockets

hemlock poisonous plant with small white flowers

hydrogen lightest of all pure chemical substances, a gas that easily catches fire

inhaler device used for breathing in medicines through the mouth or nose

insane very sick state of mind

laboratory scientific work place for experiments, called a "lab"

mercury heavy poisonous metal (also called quicksilver) that is liquid at room temperature

nitroglycerine oily, explosive, poisonous liquid used to make dynamite

ozone layer gas layer high above Earth that blocks out most of the Sun's harmful ultraviolet (UV) rays

pesticide chemical used to kill harmful pests, especially insects such as flies or beetles

petrochemical chemical obtained from oil (petroleum) or natural gas

phosphorus poisonous yellowish, white, or red substance that shines in the dark and catches fire easily in air

polymer substance made of many identical chemical units linked together

potassium soft, silver-white, lightweight metal that catches fire if it touches water

pressure pressing force that tries to push or squeeze

respiration when living things breathe in oxygen and release carbon dioxide

shock wave sudden burst of energy that travels very quickly

stroke sudden illness caused by lack of blood to the brain, usually due to a blood clot

urine waste liquid passed out of the body, usually pale yellow

vaccine injection to produce protection or immunity to a particular disease

Index

acids 5, 9, 16, 35, 46
air 12, 13
alchemy 10, 11, 32, 49
anesthetics 20, 21, 22, 23, 24, 25, 35
antiseptics 22, 23
Aristotle 9, 13
aspirin 46

Baekeland, Leo 43
Bakelite 42, 43
balloons 14, 15
Boyle, Robert 12–13, 14
Brand, Hennig 32, 33
breathing 16, 17
Bunsen, Robert 27

carbon 28
carbon dioxide 16, 17
Cavendish, Henry 14–15
cellophane 43
chemical warfare 38–39
chemical weapons 40, 41
chemotherapy 47
chlorine 39, 40
chloroform 21, 24, 25

da Vinci, Leonardo 38
Davy, Humphry 18, 19, 30, 31
Dulong, Pierre 30–31
dyes 6, 7, 49
dynamite 36, 37

elements 9, 13, 26
ether 22, 23, 24, 25, 35

explosions 28, 30, 35, 36–37, 38

Faraday, Michael 27, 31
fermenting 7, 17
Finkelstein, David 49
fire 6, 7, 26–27, 32, 38
fuels 26, 44

gases 4, 5, 6, 28, 38
    anesthetics 20–25
    breathing 16–17
    hydrogen 14–15
    in air 12–13
    laughing gas 18–19
    poisonous 40–41
glass 26, 27
gold 7, 10, 11, 12
gunpowder 28, 29, 30, 35

hydrogen 14, 15

laughing gas 20–21
Lavoisier, Antoine 4, 16, 17
lead 11, 25
Liston, Robert 22, 23
Long, Crawford 22
Luminol 48

magic 6, 10–11
matches 32, 33, 34, 35
mercury 7, 12
metals 6, 7, 9, 11, 26, 27
mustard gas 40

nitric acid 15
nitroglycerine 36–37
nitrogen 13
nitrous oxide 17, 18–19, 21
Nobel, Alfred 36, 37
nylon 43, 44

oil 42, 44
oxygen 13, 14, 16, 17, 26

Parkes, Alexander 42
petrochemicals 42
phosphorus 32, 33, 34, 35
plastics 42, 43, 44–45, 49
polymers 44
pottery 6, 7, 26, 27
Priestley, Joseph 16, 17, 18

Scheele, Carl 16, 17
Schonbein, Christian 35
Schwarz, Berthold 28, 29
Simpson, James 24–25
Socrates 8
surgery 23, 24, 45

Walker, John 33
water 4, 14, 30
weapons 28, 38, 39, 40
Wells, Horace 20–21